CW00823319

This book and the information contained he
purposes only. The information in this book is uistiibutcu on un. . .
Is" basis, without warranty. The author makes no legal claims,
express or implied, and the material is not meant to substitute legal
or financial counsel.

Copyright 2023 Timothy Forrest
All Rights Reserved
Published by Island Sunrises Press, 1071 S. Patrick Drive #372245,
Satellite Beach, FL 32937
Printed in the United States of America
Cover Design: Kate Nteli/Aikaterini

For Traci, Sarah, Rhiannon, Hunter,
John, Adam, Katen, and Nathan.

FOREWORD

"Tim, I don't need a recipe to sell cookies. Everyone's got a recipe" exclaimed Famous Amos founder, Wally Amos! He then proceeded to give me his secret recipe without concern and began discussing promotion, distribution and consumers.

I've known Wally for decades. His comment was an epiphany and an original principle that has been important to inform my later insights and the 5 success ingredients that are shared in this work.

In my food career both inside (25th anniversary at Tim Forrest Consulting) and outside of consulting, I've always found the backstage operations of fast-growing food companies to be much more interesting than what is usually visible to consumers or buyers - the real product origin, how the product is manufactured and distributed, syndicated category and share data, and successful management of sales and marketing efforts.

The innovative ways that Food Makers of these fast-growing companies run and market their food businesses are profound and are much more robust than a special recipe or better tasting product. The innovations must span all areas of the food business, from finding partners and copackers to channel and customer decision making to sales, marketing and more.

In the proven formula insights that follow, there are three things you will notice.

First, this book is intended to be read by food makers, entrepreneurs and brand owners. The perspective taken in this book is from the leaders seat - seeing how all the parts of a successful food company align and fit together.

Second, this book covers multiple disciplinary areas in its nature. It does not describe how each department lead in manufacturing, marketing, sales, and shipping should run their respective area. Instead, it covers how, from the food makers or brand owners perspective, the top vital aspects of these areas should connect and work together. Each area of a Food Company is like a piece of a giant jigsaw puzzle. You'll find that this work focuses much of the time on the overlapping points between the pieces.

Third, I've distilled these success observations into a simple 5 part system that can be used by Food Makers or brand owners in any category of the store. While I've worked with plenty if not most of the product categories represented in retail stores and online, the ideas in this work can create success in any category of product.

Anytime you combine the massive dollars spent on food in this country, with the ease of bringing products to market and the lack of intellectual property protections beyond trade-dress, you are going to find an unbelievably hyper-competitive environment. It's possibly the most competitive market in the world.

Food companies that succeed in this retail environment are built, by necessity, to use systems and processes that you'll soon read and discover. There is no option. The path that leads to success is proven and essential for long-term survival in this business.

The big opportunity for you is to take this recipe and apply it to your food business products, categories and channels. "God gives you the sight, the right, and the might to do great things, but you have to develop the fight!" It's my hope that this book is the recipe you use in your food company fight to challenge the category status quo, shatter your growth goals and achieve remarkable food revenue success.

Tim Forrest

CONTENTS

CHAPTER ONE

The Ultimate Food Money Machine

The success of the Food Money Machine is a direct outcome of creating smart decisions, leading a talented team, and keeping everyone focused on getting the right things done. Food Money Machine growth is not an accident; it's the result of deliberate thoughts, behaviors, and actions. Growth is within your control.

The Food Money Machine takes the market into account while creating methods and processes that scale. The key is to develop sustainable processes and systems for value duplication and growth in your current and home market.

Without regard to local or regional financial and business health, too often food entrepreneurs will dream of adding new markets and channels to fix poor strategy, mend the absence of demand and offer support to a weak market position. They desperately think the addition of more locations will quickly increase growth and provide a channel for their product's deficiency.

The market and revenue growth that your Food Money Machine experiences (or doesn't experience) is a direct consequence of your decisions and actions:

You decide which categories you will compete in.

✓   You decide which products and claims to offer your consumers.

✓   You decide the markets and cities you will serve

✓   You decide on which food growth channels you'll use to fuel your company's growth.

✓   You decide who's on your team.

At the end of the day, you decide everything.

Three key decisions you need to make to achieve Food Money Machine growth:

1. Choose the right growth food product opportunities to pursue and select the right approach for each channel.

2. Manage growth by standardizing your operations and developing business processes that can handle a much larger number of customers than you currently serve now.

3. Sustain growth by using a disciplined system to manage your growth portfolio, build your team, and maintain accountability for results.

Let me emphasize, just because something appears to be simple doesn't mean it's necessarily going to be easy to carry out. The devil is very much in the details and if you are in the food or CPG business today, you already have come to face this fact. Let's discuss the Food Money Machine—the foundation of all growth.

Your Food Money Machine Recipe

FOOD MONEY MACHINE	**THE FOOD MONEY MACHINE IS BUILT UTILIZING FIVE NECESSARY INGREDIENTS:**	**recipe for riches**
PREP TIME:	1. Target consumers who are aware of their problem.	
TOTAL TIME:	2. A promise that your product makes to prospective consumers.	
The Food Money Machine is the specific market opportunity combined with your company's food product approach to capturing it.	3. Add a distribution channel for reaching and transacting with the target shopper. 4. Provide a product that fulfills the promise made to the consumer. 5. For long-term growth, Add a sustainable competitive advantage.	

FROM TIM'S KITCHEN.
TIMFORREST.COM
WWW.FOODMONEYMACHINE.COM

The foundation of revenue food growth, in every company, is the Food Money Machine. A Food Money Machine is a specific market opportunity combined with your company's food product approach for capturing it.

The Food Money Machine is built utilizing five ingredients:

1. A target consumer who's aware of his or her problem.

2. A promise that your product makes to prospective consumers.

3. A distribution channel for reaching and transacting with the target shopper.

4. A product that fulfills the promise made to the consumer.

5. A sustainable competitive advantage.

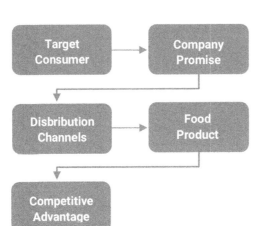

Although this appears simple and familiar, most food companies don't implement these key elements correctly. And even if one time these elements are aligned successfully, long term success isn't sustainable.

Be aware: what's required for growth and mastering the subtleties of what's required for growth are two different things. Each can have dramatically different impact on revenue.

For example, while most food entrepreneurs are aware of these key issues, many tackle them in the wrong order. Often, they will focus on product development before gaining a thorough understanding of their target consumer, determining the right food product promise, and selecting an effective food distribution channel. They make these mistakes and wonder why their food company isn't growing. Again, the details matter.

In this recipe book for success, I'll provide an overview of the key concepts based on my experience.

The Target Customer

The foundation of a Food Money Machine is a target consumer who:

1. Has a problem.
2. Is aware of their problem.
3. Has the ability and desire to pay to solve their problem.

If the consumer has a problem and doesn't recognize it, there is no sale. You likely will not sell artisan grass-fed beef to a consumer on a vegan food regimen. You can participate in multiple market size exercises to determine the size of consumer markets for almost any problem today. Plus, by studying market forecasting models, you can predict how many consumers will likely have the problem in the future. These are actions you should be taking, but for our Food Money Machine, you have to remember this: no problem, no sale.

The second hurdle is your target consumer's level of awareness about their problem. A consumer doesn't spend money solving a problem they don't realize they have. Natural Products Expo happens each year on both coasts. Every state between the coasts is littered with food companies that crash and burn trying to solve a problem that their target customer didn't realize they had.

It's extremely easier to solve a consumer's known problem than to solve a problem they don't realize exists. The reason is financial. If your consumer isn't currently aware of their problem, you have to invest your marketing resources to teach them about their problem. This approach leaves you no resources to convince the shopper to buy from your company.

The third hurdle is discovering if the consumer cares enough about the problem to pay to solve it. If the shopper doesn't care, they won't buy. You can try to force them to care. But, if at some fundamental level they don't, there's nothing you can do about it. Instead, go find another consumer segment to target or a different problem to solve.

You'd be surprised how many food company startups and product launches at larger companies, fail to overcome this basic hurdle. They attempt to solve a problem they believe the customer should care about. But what the company fails to recognize is, just because they think a consumer should care, doesn't mean they actually do. Once again, the details matter.

Along these same lines, you must consider if the market dynamics will allow you to:

1. Introduce your product to the category,

2. Solve the problem.

3. Make a profit.

Also, is there space in the market and on shelves for your product?

Can you economically succeed serving the consumer in your chosen category?

For you to succeed, your consumer has to pay to play. If they aren't willing to pay money for your food or beverage item, unfortunately, you will not experience growth.

The Promise: Is it Credible, Compelling and Unique?

The second component of the Food Money Machine is the promise you make to your consumers to persuade them to buy. This component is frequently overlooked, or its importance is grossly under-estimated.

The key to get a shopper to buy is to offer a promise that:

1. Is different (or at least different enough) from the competition.

2. Provides a genuinely compelling benefit.

3. Has credibility.

The promise is what gets the consumer to buy. Most people (especially chefs) find this idea troublesome and are conflicted by it. They expect a consumer to buy because of the product's unique flavor and nutritional value. At the end of the day, a consumer doesn't really want or need a particular food product; they only buy based on the promise of how they'll benefit from the food product.

For example, nobody buys a dozen eggs because they only want raw in-shell eggs; they want a satisfying breakfast or a delicious cake to share with friends and family.

Another example is the mom who invests in the nutrient-rich formula for her baby. She is not buying the formula because she likes it; she's buying it because she needs to know her baby is receiving the best nutrition possible that promotes great health. The truth is she won't know if the product is really a better purchase. So, she buys on the promise of a perceived health and nutrition benefit for her baby.

This quote sums up the point: "The role of the promise is to get customers to buy. The role of the product is to keep the customer satisfied after the sale and to keep you from being called a liar."

This is the underlying reason why an inferior tasting product will often outsell a superior one (much to the frustration of the food makers who created the better tasting item). A consumer often doesn't know the difference between two products unless they buy and use both items. Since most consumers only buy one product, they never experience for themselves which one is better. Instead, they simply choose whichever company offers a better price, a familiar brand, or a more credible promise.

Distribution Channels: If You Don't Reach Customers, Everything Else Is Irrelevant

Once you have a target consumer in mind and have found a promise that works, you're ready for the next step in creating a Food Money Maker. You need to find or create one or more distribution channels to reach your target shopper.

How you intend to distribute your food product needs to be determined (or at least considered) prior to product development.

You will likely need to modify your product to make it more compatible with your chosen distribution channel (i.e., club stores, convenience stores, restaurants, retail stores, stadiums, online channels, direct, and natural channel).

Here is a simple example: Your initial food product, along with production and the various flavor variations and recipes, is packaged for a variety of channels and retail environments. If the product is sold in club stores, we know the buyers demand special packaging and a display pallet that markets your brand. In convenience stores, the product is single portion and for immediate consumption. Does the consumer prefer shelf-stable or a refrigerated, fresh option?

Another example comes from an incredibly talented chef, holder of a Grand Diplôme® from Le Cordon Bleu in Paris. By changing the name from Charlie's Fine Foods (long story, but Charlie was not his name) to a more brand compatible message, the chef gained national television exposure and commercially published a recipe book with Penguin Random House bearing the new name.

In short, the company created their product before they decided on their distribution channels and their optimal con-sumer. They built a very useful product but couldn't deliver it to their target customer.

In the end, too many food companies crash and burn, in spite of having a better product. They design food products that aren't compatible with the distribution channels they attempt to use. As a rule of thumb, you can't just build an easy-to-use, great tasting product. You must also deliberately create a food product that is compatible for selling through the distribution channels you select. It's a small, but absolutely necessary detail.

The Food Product

Now it's time to create a food product or beverage. Once a customer buys on the promise of a major benefit, it's the role of the product to deliver on said promise. This results in a happy, satisfied and returning shopper.

In the Food Money Machine system, the product development step occurs late in the process for a deliberate reason. The product must be designed to meet the promises made to consumers, which generates revenue, and be compatible with the distribution channel needed to reach the shopper.

By starting the product development process too early, you aren't aware of which promises consumers are willing to pay for and which distribution channel factors you need to consider.

This is a significant departure from how product development is approached in many foods startup companies. In these companies, you'll hear a lot about:

- Ingredients
- Certifications
- Specifications

In most cases, these requirements are concerned with how the product will be used by the consumer. My argument is that development efforts should include meeting the requirements of the selling channel and not just the product usage process.

Sustainable Competitive Advantage

Creating food revenue growth doesn't mean you will sustain that growth. Generating extreme revenue growth has a habit of getting the attention of prospective competitors, which encourages them to come and compete with you as evidenced in Spins or IRI scan data.

The lifespan of a Food Money Maker depends entirely on what competitive advantages your company possesses and uses in conjunction with that particular growth engine. A competitive advantage is a physical or intangible asset that gives you an advantage over the competition.

A physical asset might be having the largest sales force, direct-to-store distribution network, or in-market warehouse network in your segment. Intangible assets are things like a rare food patent, brand reputation, or an exclusive partnership with a much larger CPG company.

The more difficult an advantage is for a category competitor to duplicate, the more sustainable the advantage. By deliberately linking a growth engine to one or more competitive advantages, you'll be able to sustain revenue from that engine for a longer period of time. An endeavor that isn't easy in the food space.

Creating a New Growth Engine with Minimal Effort

When you put these five ingredients together in a food business—a target consumer, a company promise, a distribution channel, a product, and a sustainable competitive advantage—you have a Food Money Maker. Too many food leaders in the product-centered food world, tend to equate food revenue growth opportunities with a product development project. The only problem with that approach is that it leaves so much money on the table. Often, it's much easier to make simple adjustments—to your target consumer, to your promise, or to your distribution channel—than it is to change your one item with your food product.

Here's an example in building a Food Money Maker but not focusing exclusively on developing a new food product. Jell-O has been around for more than 100 years and you can find it in most stores that sell food. Founded in the 1800's, the product has changed minimally from its origin and very few new flavors have been added over the years.

Lime Jell-O is considered the best-selling flavor and is found on the shelves in multiple channels and numerous grocery stores for under $1 for the ubiquitous 3-ounce box. Kraft Heinz Company changed the container size and label to create an entirely new product: Jell-O Unicorn Slime in a 14.8-ounce resealable container. The "new" product retails for $5.49 per unit.

The manufacturer, Kraft Heinz Company, applied a bit of creativity with a simple change to the promise and labeling, then transferred the product from the food track into the toy and gift channel!

The sales have been dramatic for this edible gelatin mix. It's primarily a new colorful label in a round container which increased the retail by almost 500%!

Distribution isn't a key concern because Jell-O knew they could leverage their existing supermarket relationships to get a "slime toy" offering on the shelves, giving them a competitive advantage.

In manufacturing, they use the same lines that make the Jell-O product. The only difference is in the very last step of the manufacturing process. They simply change the container and label on the product to one that now features the new Unicorn and ship in the new master case.

To illustrate this point, one more example is consumer-packaged goods. Several years ago, heart disease researchers discovered that taking a baby aspirin every day could significantly reduce the chances of a heart attack (I am not a medical professional nor am I providing medical advice).

Armed with this knowledge, Bayer decided to create a growth engine to capitalize on this opportunity. They decided to target consumers concerned about their heart attack risk. This wasn't the same audience as those concerned about getting rid of headaches, aches, or pains. So, the first step taken in creating this new growth engine involved targeting a different type of consumer.

They simply created a new promise in their advertising and on their product label. They promised that taking a low-dose aspirin every day could lower the risk of a heart attack and backed their promise up with the research.

Next, they introduced a low-dosage aspirin they described as the "exact same dosage" used in the clinical research study to demonstrate a small dose of aspirin every day could reduce the chance of a heart attack. In reality, all they did was take the baby aspirin product and change the label to support this new promise. No new production changes, no product research or manufacturer development work was required.

Even though the original research on using aspirin to prevent heart attacks was first published in 1989, the product is still on the shelves of local supermarket and drugstores nationwide resulting in millions of dollars in sales. Exceedingly impressive revenues resulted from simply changing a label. Amazing, isn't it?

These examples illustrate by simply tweaking the recipe of one or more of the five Food Money Machine ingredients, you can create a new growth engine for your company.

Key Ideas:

- All revenue growth starts with the target consumer, who has a problem that needs to be solved.

- To get a shopper to buy, you must make them a promise that is unique, credible and compelling.

- Distribution is critical because, without it, your prospects will never see your product.

- Design products to be easy to sell (i.e., compatible with your distribution channel) and to fulfill expectations set with the customer.

- The lifespan of your revenue growth engine depends on the sustainability of your competitive advantage.

CASE STUDY

New Channel Nearly Doubles Sales Revenue

Tim repeatedly doubles revenues within the first year for clients. It often is a simple process of reviewing the foundational five ingredients and selecting the most likely lever.

For Sir James Dyson and his UK technology and vacuum company Tim sought effectiveness and opportunity in new channels.

When approached by Dyson's business development specialist, Tim was intrigued with the idea of helping their division that focused on restaurants achieve massive growth and found it in a new distribution channel. In the first year, the effort achieved 83% growth from this one channel observation.

Initially, Tim requested that Dyson send all invoices for the prior sales period. After review and much to his surprise the largest order came from a healthcare location. Tim immediately built a database of all hospitals and healthcare facilities and emailed it out for the team. The list generated massive growth and success and the single-largest new account the following year!

Simple actions based on hard to see insights are the five building blocks of food maker.

CHAPTER TWO:

Consumers Define Innovation

The Food Money Machine is the foundation of all food growth. A revenue growth engine is a specific market opportunity combined with your company's innovative approach for capturing it.

The consumer is always left out of building new food products. Many food companies rely upon recipe, special ingredients, product claims and packaging to highlight and drive innovation which results in failure after failure. Inez Blackburn, professor at The University of Toronto, highlights this fact stating 80% of new food products introduced into supermarkets fail.

The Food Money Machine Consists of Five Key Ingredients:

1. A target consumer who's aware of his or her problem.

2. A promise that your company makes to prospective shoppers.

3. A distribution channel for reaching and transacting with the target consumer.

4. A food or beverage product that fulfills the promise it made to the consumer.

5. A sustainable competitive advantage.

The first step in creating a Food Money Machine seems simple. Start with the person who has the money: the shopper. Figure out what the consumer wants, but is not getting elsewhere, and give it to them. A slightly better tasting product is unsustainable for building a new food business or generate extraordinary food revenue success.

However, because something is simple doesn't always imply it's easy to do. The failure rates drive this point home. In this article, we examine the common problems related to identifying and knowing your target food shopper. The use of real-world food examples will illustrate how to tackle these challenges.

All of the problems listed in the troubleshooting section of this article result in a common, highly visible symptom: No revenue growth. While the lack of revenue growth is a single, visible symptom, it has dozens of potential causes.

The following are a small sample of the most common problems and their solutions.

1. Consumer Target Failure:

You're Guessing (Incorrectly) About What the Target Consumer Wants.

A common problem that occurs in most startup food companies, and in new divisions of larger food companies, is the company doesn't have a clear understanding of the target consumer. I have a simple acid test that I use to determine how well an organization knows their target shopper: I ask them to show me a listing of the consumers that have purchased or trialed the product and their responses or feedback. I'm seeking external verification of consumer demand.

You'd be surprised how often I am unable to get any consumer feedback referencing the new food product. I use this test because the attempt to create a new revenue growth engine is often based on incorrect information. If you don't have accurate information about what you're aiming for, you can't hit the target. The bigger the company, the bigger the mistaken features of innovation. Here's the key to getting accurate information about target consumers: Talk to your consumers and the more the better.

One of the reasons I enjoy working with small food entrepreneurs is I get to interview them and ask about their process for starting their business and marketing their best products. Their responses instantly scream to me and divide the winners from the losers. I'm searching for those products and leaders that have market success regardless of the size or scale. If they have a single successful retail location of shoppers, we often can land thousands more.

One of my retail clients, a top 10 global retailer, struggled repeatedly with a new product category in dairy. They had been introducing a niche product with a huge lack of success and downright product failure. Initially, the product was expected to be a tremendous hit with shoppers.

With my shopper insight, the buyer agreed and accepted our product formulation that more precisely delivered on what shoppers were looking for in the category. The buyer went with our specification changes and adjusted their retail set with our product that was fitted to consumer tastes and expectations. Sales were explosive! The product went on to produce more than $100 million in sales.

The results were extraordinary and the resulting success was driven by shopper tastes and desires.

While the company had achieved some revenues with their recipe and product claims, it had not maximized its revenue potential. It pays to know what your target consumer desires and not assume what they want.

2. Consumer Target Failure:

Target Shoppers Don't Want to Buy What You Want to Sell.

Another very common problem is that the target shopper doesn't want to buy what you want to sell. Ironically, this really isn't a target shopper problem—it's your company's problem.

At the end of the day, you can't make your consumers want something they don't want or need. When there is an underlying desire, you can use sales and marketing to sharpen demand and increase the customer's sense of urgency to solve their problem. But, no matter how savvy you are, you can't make customers want something they don't care about.

There's a saying: *"A great salesperson can sell ice to Eskimos."* I may slip and call it idiotic marketing, but it actually ignores the facts. A great marketer or food marketing entrepreneur realizes it's a lot smarter to sell hot soup or coffee to Eskimos than ice.

Ask yourself if you currently have food growth engines in your portfolio that are metaphorically attempting to sell ice to Eskimos. Remember, food companies exist to supply products and services that consumers demand. Unfortunately, it does not work as well when you try to supply food products you hope customers will demand.

3.   Consumer Target Failure

Target Consumer Has a Problem, But Not a Severe Problem

Sometimes, your assumption that a target consumer has a problem is correct. But, in the eyes of the consumer, if the problem is not severe enough, they have no sense of urgency in regard to solving the problem.

This is a tougher case because you have to make an assessment as to whether the urgency is likely to increase (e.g., future demand for vegan ice cream, carbon-neutral broccoli) or if the problem is basically not important to the shopper.

If the consumer's problem will indefinitely be modest in nature, this limits the potential revenue of the food growth engine you're considering.

What you decide to do next is somewhat dependent on:

- The other growth engines you have in your portfolio

- Their maturity levels

- And the resources required by each one.

Generally speaking, I would suggest that you start looking for alternative growth opportunities.

4. Consumer Target Failure

Failing to Recognize that Adjacent Shopper Categories Are Growing Faster than the One You're Currently Targeting.

Most food categories are fairly dynamic and continually evolving, and it's often difficult to spot the completely hidden growth opportunity. Identifying this opportunity, before anyone else does, is only half the equation; you must also capture it ahead of the market. People do it, but it's tough. (Fortunately, my clients are often champions in this regard.)

Equally important, but much easier, is recognizing when a competitor has successfully tapped into a new consumer segment adjacent to the section you're targeting.

An example of this comes from the apple sauce category. Manufacturers did not recognize the early trend of portable foods. They didn't see moms were spending more time commuting with kids and eating in the car. GoGo Squeeze recognized this trend and built a portable apple sauce solution that sells over half a billion pouches a year.

Over a decade ago, the category of yogurt competitors failed to recognize how Chobani built an entire segment with their Greek yogurt offering, resulting in massive category disruption for yogurt makers. It was a fast-growing segment missed by the other yogurt makers, until many years later. It propelled Chobani into a billion-dollar player.

Here's the lesson: You must pay attention to your competitor's growth engines, particularly the ones that work. This close observation will identify potential growth opportunities for your company.

5.   Consumer Target Failure:

Not Recognizing that Your Existing Shoppers May Be Different from the Newer Shoppers You Want to Target.

For companies that have been around for years, you'll often find that buyers of legacy branded food products aren't always the same buyers of future food products. It's important to keep the two distinguishable, particularly if your company has gone through some major product evolutions. If you look at the market results, companies are ignoring new shoppers.

An example of this is realizing that your legacy branded ketchup buyers may not be the same buyers for your natural hummus dip. A more recent version of this would be recognizing that your Oreo and Tang buyers might not be the buyers of plant-based all-natural protein bars.

Here's the general rule: Yesterday's target consumer may not be tomorrow's target consumer.

Closing Thoughts

All target consumer problems discussed in this section highlight two distinct points:

- You need to be familiar with your consumer's wants, needs, desires and problems.

- Recognize when a new type of shopper is emerging.

At the end of the day, the consumer is the foundation of all successful food businesses, so you need to think about them early and often.

Key Ideas:

- All revenue growth opportunities start with getting to know the person with the money, your shopper.

- No amount of marketing will convince your consumers to desire something they don't want or need.

- Adjust your target consumer over time to adapt to changing markets and to create new opportunities for your food company.

CASE STUDY

$150 MILLION EXIT

The charge was to effectively review and optimize distribution channels to consumers and engage market teams, while driving consumer and profit success. Tim reviewed existing processes and developed new channel programs to achieve turnaround success for a four-plant division, resulting in highly profitable $150 million sale of the division.

CHAPTER 3:

Food Money Machine - Brand Promise

The Food Money Machine is the foundation of all growth. A Food Money Machine is a specific market opportunity combined with your company's approach to capturing it.

A Food Money Machine Consists of Five Key Ingredients:

1. A target consumer who's aware of his or her problem.

2. A promise that your company makes to prospective shoppers.

3. A distribution channel for reaching and transacting with the target consumer.

4. A food product that fulfills the promise made to the consumer.

5. A sustainable competitive advantage.

After selecting a target consumer, the second step is to determine what promise you'll make to get them to buy. The ideal promise is one that is unique, compelling, and credible.

There's a reason why each of these steps is essential: If your promise is not unique, there is no incentive for a shopper to pick your company over any other competitor. If a legitimate difference does exist between you and your competitors' promises, your promise should clearly indicate that difference. Otherwise, there is no differentiation in the mind of the shopper.

Actual product differences matter only if they help you differentiate the promise you make to your consumers. This is a subtle but vital distinction.

This leads to our second point. Consumers don't buy products; they buy what a product does for them. In other words, consumers buy based on their perception of how a product will benefit them. Your promise must offer a compelling benefit. If the promise is not compelling, you are, in effect, promising to solve a problem your customer doesn't really care about.

Finally, you need to make your promise credible. In many markets, buyers are extremely skeptical. They assume all companies are liars (or at least exaggerators). When you combine this skepticism with the common complaint that "all those companies sound the same," buyers don't know who to buy from and end up choosing randomly or on price.

There are several key problems that arise when developing a unique, compelling, and credible promise. Let's look at the most common problems and your options for addressing them.

Problem #1:

Your Promise is not Unique (or not Unique Enough) Compared to Your Competition

This is probably the number one problem I see in food companies, and here's why knowing about it is so important. Providing a dramatically different promise, even if your product is similar to the products offered by your competition, forces the customer to consider what you're offering in more detail. If your promise sounds the same as your competitors' promises, your offer gets lumped together with your competitors' offers.

There are numerous tools at your disposal for making your promise unique. There's absolutely no excuse for failing to improve the differentiation of your promise in your channel.

Consider Promising the Polar Opposite of What the Competition Is Promising.

If the rest of the pack promises the lowest prices, consider promising the highest price in your category—and then figure out what the heck you have to include in your product to justify the higher price.

If the rest of your category promises customers organic or all-natural features, consider promising "fresh and local-grown." Your promise then becomes: "We use only the freshest and local-grown ingredients."

If the rest of the competition promises the fastest home delivery in the pizza industry, consider promising the slowest (but 200% tastier) home delivery in the industry.

This technique is based on the "Zig-Zag" principle. If everyone else decides to "zig," then you consider "zagging" instead. Of course, you will need to carefully consider this strategy before employing it— sometimes it makes sense and at other times it doesn't. However, here's the general rule of thumb: Any time there's an opportunity to be the polar opposite of your competition it's worth taking a hard look to see if it makes sense.

Be Number One in Your Industry at Something, Even if It Means Being Mediocre at Everything Else

In a cluttered marketplace, there's no benefit to being the same as everyone else. If everyone else offers average quality and average service at an average price, you're much better off picking one of the three in which to lead your industry. This means that you must also be willing to risk sacrificing the other elements of your promise.

You are better off being the company offering the highest quality in town but with absolutely no service at the highest prices than offering something middle of the road. You will certainly alienate a large portion of your category but will attract a narrower segment that values quality more than anything else.

The idea here is that you have to be dramatically better than your competition—at something—to warrant the attention of prospective buyers. A related rule of thumb is that it's good to be either loved or hated because "no one makes money being average or just polite."

Solve a Bigger Problem

When a food leader is struggling for ideas to make a promise more unique, I can always rely on the strategy of solving a bigger problem, because it works in any market situation. The gist of this strategy is to solve a problem that is bigger than what your industry is accustomed to solving on behalf of consumers.

By expanding the problem to be solved, you instantly open up ways to distinguish your promise in your category. Let's look at a few food and beverage examples to drill this point home.

In the candy market, all of the candy players are slugging it out over who can be better, cheaper, more outlandish, co-brand with the latest cartoon, and introduce new brand partnerships in hope of driving more sales. However, my friend David Klein (founder and inventor of Jelly Belly Jelly Beans) made a brilliant strategic decision to "solve a bigger problem" that skyrocketed sales for Spectrum Confections.

Klein created and introduced the world's first CBD Jelly Bean that globally shook the candy and news world with his functional beans. David realized that people really wanted relief from various physical symptoms. The jelly bean with CBD was the perfect dosage vehicle for the popular therapeutic ingredient. David solved a much bigger issue for consumers and he's been rewarded leaving competitors in the dust.

The underlying technique for solving a bigger problem involves two simple steps: First, look at the things the customer purchases before and after they buy your product; and second, look at the activities the customer engages in before and after they buy your product. Using this "before and after" analysis, you can identify all the possible options for "solving a bigger problem."

In David Kleins example, he realized the dosage metric per jelly bean would be a tremendous benefit to consumers and elevated the jelly bean from candy to remedy.

Unfortunately, the other candy companies missed it because they defined their business around the products they manufacturer and retailers sold – candy. By focusing on this narrow definition of the problem, they missed the opportunity to solve a bigger chunk of the customer's larger problem.

While David's CBD Jelly Beans provide an example involved in the major shift in industry boundaries, there are much simpler examples that follow the same "solve a bigger problem" idea.

Let's say your company manufactures laundry detergent. An example of "solving a bigger problem" would be to automatically ship the consumer refills or new containers of detergent each month or quarter. You instantly shift your customer promise from delivering "a quality wash" to delivering a lifetime of stress-free clean clothes without having to ever run out of detergent again. This is one method to set you apart from your competition. To solve an even bigger problem for washer and dryer buyers, you might offer clothes washer equipment makers a free 90-day "laundry detergent" subscription that automatically rolls them into a monthly auto-ship replenishment program for their buyers.

This solves the customer's headache of having to continually pick-up or re-order detergent from the store. Remember, customers don't want detergent; they want nice looking and clean clothes. If you're in the "nice looking clothes for life" business, you realize that your consumers are going to have to re-order detergent dozens of times over the next 10 years. Why not solve the customer's "bigger problem" from the outset, with a single purchasing decision?

Would such a promise work? I have no idea—you'd have to test it and Amazon is on it today. However, I do know that it's a unique promise with a compelling benefit. Because of this uniqueness, customers will pay more attention to it than if you make the same promise everyone else is making.

Regardless of whether a consumer loves or hates a unique promise, they are forced to stop and consider it; they can't simply continue with their autopilot mentality that rejects all vendors because they seem to be completely identical.

Solve a Bigger Problem by Bundling Third-Party Products with Yours

What happens if you don't have the staff to support "free" samples for your product, or you don't have product development capacity for creating add-on products, or even additional features?

In these situations, you can still "solve a bigger problem" by pre-bundling the commonly used accessories consumers typically buy with your product. Even if you buy these third-party products at retail prices, the simple convenience of a single package will be appealing to your consumers.

This approach is like the difference between selling coffee beans and selling a coffee making home kit like the Keurig with pouches. A kit may include a starter assortment of coffees, machine, cups, flavors, and serving accessories. This solves a "bigger problem" for the customer—eliminating the need to evaluate other products in related categories and to research compatibility issues. It's all done for them.

In many grocery deli departments, retailers sell "solution meal specials" that are often joint-marketed by alliance partners. Pre-bundling is based on the same idea. Instead of promising the consumer only the benefits of your component, you can promise the benefits of the entire solution set. You can do this even if the other components of the solution come from other suppliers.

Niche the Promise to a More Targeted Customer

Another technique for beefing up the uniqueness of your promise is to target the promise to a more focused audience. For example, if you sell a supplement or vitamin, simply add the words "for Moms" or "for children" to your promotional materials.

If you sell coffee with various extra amounts of caffeine, you might add the words "for students" or "for computer workers." You can validate the promise with an argument that extra caffeine keeps you alert, and the coffee is specially designed for your target consumer's needs.

Coke has even started using this technique over the past few years with their names on the label of Coca-Cola products. Interestingly, they offered 100's of peoples given names and consumers would search for their name or friends name on the package while the product inside was unchanged and yielded massive sales results.

Sometimes, creating a niche version of a product only requires superficial changes. Often, much of the niche-specific different-iation can come from simple label changes, suggesting target markets, or defining new and clever uses for a product.

Multi-Niche the Promise to Multiple Targeted Customers

The niche strategy is not just a technique relegated to smaller companies. Large companies can use the same technique—with a twist. Instead of targeting a single niche, you can multi-niche your products by targeting multiple niches. You would simply have multiple "editions" of your product that would enable you to make the promise that "this edition was made specifically with your needs in mind."

You could create dozens of editions, with perhaps minor (or no) differences in features, that would support making more specialized promises. For some people, this may seem a bit sneaky or devious. Allow me to explain why this is not the case and, in fact, is a significant consumer benefit in both perception and reality.

Let's go back to the vitamins targeted for kids. At first, this just seems like wordplay. In reality, the words make a difference to the consumer. The Mom knows the product is safe for her kids and has the nutrients that she is looking for in a multi-vitamin. Mom knows it will work for her for her kids and is happy.

Even if your product functionally serves a wide range of users, consumers don't know that. They will assume that a more specialized offering is better, more relevant, and more appropriate for them than a generic offering. More importantly, they leap to this conclusion quickly and with less comparison-shopping than if they were considering a generic product.

Problem #2:

Your Promise Offers No Compelling Benefit

If your promise offers a benefit the target consumer doesn't find compelling, this means you don't know your target consumer well enough.

You have two options here: You can keep the same target consumer and find the benefit they do care about (then change your product to support the new promise), or you can change the target consumer to one that values the promise you're already making (and keep the promise that your product is already able to back up).

Either way, the general rule of thumb here is: If you find yourself in the situation of promising the wrong benefit, back up and learn more about your target consumer before trying again.

Problem #3:

Your Promise Is Unique and Compelling, But Your Target Customer Doesn't Believe You

What if your promise is unique, and you're certain the offer is compelling, but sales are still down? This often means prospective consumers don't believe your promise. Skepticism among consumers and business-to-business customers is probably at an all-time high, while trust is at an all-time low.

To illustrate this point, walk downtown of any major city and attempt to give away $1 bills, one at a time, to people on the street. You will find it's a difficult task to accomplish. Most people will duck away and immediately start walking away from you due to skepticism. They know there is a catch and do not believe anything you might say in relation to the event.

Your target consumer is the same. He doesn't trust you or your competitors. He assumes you are lying or at least exaggerating your promises. In fact, companies that exaggerate their promises ("We're the best in the food industry" or "We're number one") is such a common practice that it's actually acknowledged by U.S. law.

As I understand it, a food company making a general boast that they're the best is called "puffery"—and it's legal. The lawmakers determined that since everyone knows companies exaggerate and nobody believes them anyway, there's no harm in letting companies exaggerate their non-numerical claims (of course this is not legal advice—please seek an attorney prior to making claims of any type). That's a pretty sad commentary on the state of skepticism, particularly in the United States.

So, how do you counter such skepticism? You must supply overwhelming proof that what you say is true. I'll list several ways you can provide this proof. At the end of the day, it is simply impossible to have too much proof.

Proof Technique #1:

Testimonials and Customer References

Hands down, the best way to provide proof to skeptical consumers is to provide them with consumer testimonials. Show them letters and notes from your happy customers. Let them watch video clips of your shoppers explaining how happy they are with your products. Invite them to attend

live, in-person event at your facility or wine tasting event with your product to meet your happy consumers.

This works equally well selling to consumers as it does to other businesses. When I was building my consulting website, I included a case study tab with many of the projects I've worked on and provided specifics – such as the first and last name of individuals we dealt with – details about their situations and concerns. It also includes information on what we worked on and statements regarding "before" and "after" financial results that demonstrates the benefits of working with us.

The reason it works so well is that it provides ample proof that well respected and well-known companies trusted my solution. We don't have to say we are the best in our market, our amazing proof makes the point for us.

Proof Technique #2:

Demonstrations and Free Demos

Another way to prove your point is with a simple demonstration. Simply demo your product to a customer or allow them to taste it for themselves. Demos work incredibly well at proving your point. If your product tastes great and better than your competition, demonstrate the product and prove it. Great food photography is a hack for sampling and can save money and time.

Costco Wholesale demo's everyday they are open. It's part of their core structure and marketing to members. You can't walk through a Costco on a Saturday and miss the many demo stations situated throughout the building. They do it, continue doing it and encourage vendors to demo (I know based on almost a $100 million in purchases for clients from Costco Wholesale.) their products due to the positive impact it has on sales and new product introductions.

Successful companies know that demos drive sales. I can look at your demo plan and tell you where success will be for your company in the next year. Demos prove your promise to consumers. The promise you decide to make has implications for how you approach product development and needs to be considered before the product is developed.

Proof Technique #3:

Increase the Specificity of Your Proof

Here's a simple way to increase the credibility of your proof. Simply increase the specificity of the proof. Let's go back to the case studies section created for my consulting website. I created it as a marketing tool for my business-to-business sales efforts. I included names, numbers, and the specific accounts for each project. I did this for an important reason: Specific details improve the credibility of the story. Specifics increase credibility.

Here's another example: Since a lot of my client work involves integrating marketing strategies with the rest of a client's operations, I'm familiar with how my efforts impact sales and revenue for various food businesses. I'm confident enough after more than 3 decades of reviewing food companies to know quickly if I can assist their growth and likely by how much.

I've been fortunate to assist many food entrepreneurs begin their food enterprises from scratch and we quickly surpass a million in sales and I've helped others quickly double sales volume of their food businesses utilizing so many of the strategies we discuss in Food Money Machine.

My experience and knowledge allow me to offer the very specific offer of $1 million in new revenue or a doubling of the business after I review your products and current position in the market. Specificity increases credibility, and credibility increases sales.

Key Ideas: The key to driving sales is to present consumers and consumers with a unique, credible promise that includes a compelling benefit. There are several ways to differentiate your company from your competitors: offer the polar opposite of what the competition is offering ("zig" when others "zag"); be #1 in your industry at something, even if you have to be dead last at everything else; solve a bigger or broader problem than your competitors are accustomed to solving; or focus on a narrower consumer segment than your competitors are willing to focus on. A more unique, more compelling, promise only drives more sales if the promise is credible. To boost the credibility of your promise, provide overwhelming proof that what you say is true through syndicated data, customer testimonials, and product tastings, trade support—and provide a highly specific detailed business case to boost the credibility of your promise.

CASE STUDY

QVC + TIM FORREST = SOLD OUT

Tim selected and placed 12 items on the direct-to-consumer channel, QVC television network nationally for clients, with exposure to 100 million households, which resulted in multiple client product sell-outs.

The key to their success with QVC was understanding the requirements of the channel and pre-planning all scripts and actions prior to going live on-air.

CHAPTER 4:

Food Money Machine - Distribution

The Food Money Machine is the foundation of all growth. A Food Money Machine is a specific consumer market opportunity combined with your company's food product to capture the market demand.

A Food Money Machine Consists of Five Key Ingredients:

1. A target consumer who's aware of his or her problem or need.

2. A promise that your company makes to prospective shoppers and consumers.

3. A distribution channel for reaching and transacting with the target shopper.

4. A food or beverage product that fulfills the promise made to the consumer.

5. A branded sustainable competitive advantage.

In this chapter, I'm going to focus on the third component: distribution channels.

Distribution (the ability to communicate and transact with a shopper) is consistently the most underestimated factor and missed opportunity in most food and beverage companies.

In my experience, distribution is more important than product development. If you have good distribution, there will be an endless line of companies wanting to partner with you to take advantage of it. The opposite, however, is much less common.

Wal-Mart doesn't manufacture a single product. It is, however, the single largest distribution channel for food and consumer packaged goods in the world. They have direct access to more customers, than any other company in the world.

In the beginning of my career, it did not occur to me the gargantuan opportunity that was before me as I learned the food business first from the loading docks and pulling food orders in warehouses. This training in distribution became the catalyst for $100's of millions in new value for multiple brands globally. Every brand needs distribution.

Nestlé leverages and has an enormous distribution channel through its retail, online, Nestle branded Amazon pages, and wholesaling partners. They've also opened new distribution capacity and invested in third-party distributors. Through these extensive relationships, Nestlé has no trouble introducing new products to consumers into these channels.

In addition, recognizing the importance of controlling distribution, Nestlé has made efforts to market directly to consumers buying direct-to-consumer brands like tails.com—bypassing third-party distribution channels.

Through its online efforts and hosted versions of all its key products, it is building direct relationships with customers on an increasingly large scale. It's all about distribution—because without it nothing happens.

The same is true with door-store-delivery only branded food companies. The largest of these companies, like Frito-Lay and Blue Bell Creameries, dominate because of their massive, installed base of customers. On-going relationships with their direct channels allow Blue Bell and other DSD operators to communicate with their customers with ease and at low cost introduce, deploy new products for tests and national roll-outs. In short, they have distribution.

When a company like Frito-Lay wants to introduce a proprietary or third-party product they can reach a surprisingly high percentage of the supermarkets, all club stores, and convenience stores in America in less than 45 days. That's the power of distribution.

In the pizza world, Dominoes, Papa Johns, and Marco's have enormous distribution power and reach. These companies have prospered, in part, because their bosses recognized that they really are in the business of distribution.

Over the past few years, Amazon.com has added food product after food product and Whole Foods to their website; providing more products for their existing shoppers to buy. (Incidentally, this is precisely what you do when you have strong distribution; you cram as many high-quality, relevant products and services as possible through your distribution system.) Amazon has capitalized on their distribution system extremely well.

The home food delivery company, Schwann's has done the same. In addition to introducing an ever-increasing array of desserts, proteins, entrees, and even seafood (Alaskan Sockeye Salmon, Vegetable Fried Rice, T-Bone Steaks, and Bagel Dogs), Schwann's has continually worked to grow its distribution—including adding UPS delivery to its network of depots and neighborhood delivery freezer trucks.

One of the reasons distribution is such an enormous asset is because of the economics of distribution. Here's how it works. Acquiring a first-time customer is expensive. If you're like most companies, 80% of your sales and marketing resources get consumed while trying to acquire new customers. These customers and their shoppers don't know you, don't trust you, and can't tell you apart from your competitors.

To get your message across, you need to blitz them with your message. Market to them, sample them, drop millions of coupons, and do whatever it takes. In contrast, you could place it on your next delivery to the store, pick up the phone or send an e-mail to your best retailers to let them know about a new product and get an order within minutes or a few weeks—depending on the category and size of the account.

So, in the distribution game, selling to a new retailer or channel is the least profitable part of the business. It's necessary, but not nearly as profitable as selling more to existing customers. The companies that are smart with distribution recognize this and are extremely focused on selling more to existing customers. I'll quote my friend John Soares. "I'd much rather sell multiple items to 500 retailers as compared to 1 item in 5,000 stores.

Dominate New Customer Acquisition by Selling More to Existing Customers.

To dominate the war for new customers the single, biggest, most unstoppable advantage is a superior ability to sell more to existing customers. This linkage isn't initially obvious to many food entrepreneurs, but if you fully appreciate this relationship, you will never look at your business in the same way again.

When a company does a good job selling to existing customers, they can afford to spend more money to acquire new customers. Taken to the extreme, this simple mathematical relationship has enormous strategic and competitive implications. If you can lead the category in sales to existing customers you will have the largest marketing war chest in your niche, bar none. This isn't a marketing theory; it's a mathematical fact.

Here's a simple example: Let's say you're trying to sell your grandfathers bbq sauce recipe bottled to Kroger and are competing against a big company like Sweet Baby Rays BBQ Sauce. Owned by Ken's Foods, they supply over 400 sku's to retailers and restaurants nationwide. In contrast, your product line might only have 3 flavors and your marketing budget is heavy on the one item.

The way the math works is Ken's can afford to invest 100 to 400 times your budget to secure any account and still make a profit, whereas you can only afford to spend based on your limited line and geographical area. In that situation, who is going to win?

When you're at a 400:1 marketing investment disadvantage it's very tough to come out ahead. Once again, this illustrates the power and importance of distribution.

Distribution is hands down one of the most important aspects of creating a Food Money Machine. It is also the factor that is consistently underestimated and is often considered only as an afterthought to food product development.

Among many food and beverage startups, the mentality is: "Let's build a product and then figure out how to sell it." Wrong! You are much better off considering how you intend to distribute a product before you build it. Before developing a product, you want to verify your assumptions about your distribution channel.

Why? For one, the food or beverage product packaging will be slightly different for almost every channel, purpose will depend on the distribution channel. It's tempting to keep distribution as an afterthought. After all, the product changes required to be compatible with distribution are often minor. However, just because the differences are minor from a development standpoint, it doesn't mean the revenue impact is minor.

When you build a product that is fundamentally incompatible with your distribution channel you can't sell it. A product is either compatible with the channel or it is not. It tends to be a binary, black or white situation rather than "maybe we can convince 'em to buy it."

Let's walk through some examples. Assume you run a snack-food company. Your company is launching a new product to be sold to your existing retailer base. To be compatible with your channels and target customers you need to provide appropriate product sizes, acceptable ingredients, existing company brand, and the right promotional offers. This will enable your existing customers to leverage your brand, their stores and consumers for your new product. This would be 100% mandatory if the product is to be compatible with any one channel. (And, with regard to creating "proof" of your promise, you'd probably want to have several documented case studies of successful retailer and consumer market success. In particular, you will need to offer each account the channel appropriate product offering for your branded food product. Otherwise, these customers won't buy.

However, if you were selling the product primarily to new consumers or new channel that don't own your branded products you might take a different approach. In this case, you might offer a new brand or better for you brand to leverage new qualities or highlight new benefits for consumers.

Different distribution channels have different requirements, which impact how the product should be developed. It's important to know this in advance and not as a last minute, "Oh darn, they won't buy this size or ingredient list."

The point is that you need to figure this out early in the process or at least consider the needs of the consumer for the specific channel.

Distribution:

A Frequently Ignored Source of Additional Revenue

There's another reason why distribution is typically under-estimated and overlooked as a major source of food revenue growth. Chefs and food product developers are notorious for a "my baby, my creation" attitude (secret recipe, family and friend favorite, unmatched flavor). The underlying belief is that we can only sell food products to our customers that we personally create. But, why?

Once you have an established, trusted relationship with a customer, you can sell all kinds of food products and even third-party packages to them. There's no need to be restricted to only those products and even categories your manufacturing plant or co-packer can produce.

If you're truly concerned about the recipe or brand reputation then don't bring in the product under their label. You might consider engaging in white labeling and private labeling their manufactured food and beverage products for your customers.

If you have even a modestly sized customer base, you can leverage your distribution channel by selling other company products and even possibly services to your customer base.

Once again, the behind-the-scenes impact of selling more in-house and third-party products to existing customers is that you can afford to invest more to acquire new customers. Your marketing budget gets larger and your ability to target consumers and new markets is improved in the process.

Now that we've gone over the basics of distribution, let's look at some common problems with distribution and how to solve them.

Distribution Problem #1:

How to Expand Self-Distributed Food Products

Solving distribution problems is easy to do conceptually, but implementing solutions is not always as easy. To expand your in-house distribution, whether it is via a direct-store-delivery team, field sales pre-sell trucks, telesales, UPS, or other method, the principle is the same.

Work relentlessly to get your in-house distribution working on a small scale in a market. Figure out what you did right. Make sure the math works, standardize it, and duplicate it.

The key to scaling up distribution is the concept I call a "repeatable unit." A repeatable unit can be a sales rep who's hitting her numbers out of the park, a marketing program that's working like crazy, or a sales script that performs unusually well. The key with a repeatable unit is that you can, well, repeat it.

So, if you have 10 salespeople and one is outselling the other nine combined, then you'd darn well better figure out what that one salesperson is doing to be effective that the others are not. Is that salesperson qualifying prospects in a different way than everyone else? What's driving the person's success? Is she more successful at getting more initial meetings with clients? If so, what's she doing that your other salespeople are not doing.

Or does that salesperson get the same number of meetings, but converts those initial meetings into closed sales at a much higher closing rate? If so, what did she do differently? You have to figure out what that person did right. You've got to break it down step-by-step. Take apart each step of the process and examine each piece separately. Try to isolate what went right.

This is similar to someone in the food plant troubleshooting or repairing some piece of production line.

They systematically check each station and step of the baking process until the problem is isolated and fixed.

I propose doing something similar, but instead of looking at this as a "troubleshooting" exercise (find the source of the trouble and fix it), look at it as a "treasure discovery" process (find out what went right so you can deliberately do more of it).

In a "treasure discovery" process you systematically isolate and check each component of the process until you isolate the primary factor that went right. This is important because if you cannot isolate what went right you cannot duplicate it on a consistent basis.

You can use this exact same process for any type of distribution channel. If you have a great marketing campaign, do a "postmortem" analysis and figure out what went right. Take the same campaign and cross-test it with a different mailing list. Take the same list and cross-test it with a different campaign. What drove the campaign's success? Was it the target audience you chose, the communication pieces, or a combination of the two?

If you got the audience right, what's the specific demo-graphic and psychographic profile of the people in that audience? Who are they? Where can you find more people exactly like them? Analytically isolate what works and duplicate it. That's the key to scaling up distribution.

Good Results Are Not Enough:

You Must Have Good Results that Can Be Duplicated

There's a big difference between achieving Food Money Maker growth temporarily or in your home market and sustaining it for decades. In the former, all your team has to focus on is generating more revenues. But, for a Food Money Maker company, delivering strong revenue growth is simply not good enough. You must have revenue growth that can be duplicated on an on-going basis.

If you can't duplicate a good result, it only means you got lucky. I don't mind having luck on my side, but I'd much rather have a proven, repeatable process. You must personally focus your team on this "duplication" aspect of revenue growth because they won't do it without your constant involvement.

You need to make this your mantra: "We don't need revenue growth; we need revenue growth that can be duplicated." That's the key to building a Food Money Machine.

Turn Growth in Distribution into a Self-Financing Activity

The other key to building a Food Money Maker is to make sure expanding distribution is a self-financing activity. Here's what I mean. Let's say you run a company that sells via a direct-store-delivery model. After extensive "treasure discovery" you've isolated and duplicated what's working well in your distribution channels. You have a "repeatable unit" in the form of a route that follows your well-honed sales system.

Let's further assume that every time you add a new truck and route, you pay $120,000 a year in overhead, the new route consistently produces $2 million in sales each year for you. How many routes do you add to your food business?

Of course, you add as many as you can finance that meet your criteria. This is an example of making expanding distribution a self-financing activity. Each time you replicate your "repeatable unit" of distribution it pays for itself, with money left over to fund the next repetition.

In this case, adding one new route generates enough revenue to pay for the next three DSD routes via margin. The new three, in turn, provide the cash flow to pay for the next four and so on. When you get the "micro-economics" of the repeatable unit to work on a small scale it makes scaling up distribution incredibly easy. This is another key for creating and sustaining a Food Money Machine.

This is also true for your supermarket business. Let's say you systematically "treasure find" your retail sales process and have gotten your numbers to a pretty good level. Your numbers show that it costs you x amount of dollars in advertising to support a market of a certain size. On average, for every new consumer that purchases your food products, your marketing budget expands by certain percentage amount of the revenue. How much should you invest in marketing? As much as you possibly can, while maintaining the quality level of the prospects you attract and your performance metrics.

In both examples expanding distribution is completely self-financed. You take a well-honed, well-understood "repeatable unit" and multiply it. The greater the difference between the costs of putting an additional repeatable unit in place and the revenue it generates, the faster you can grow, completely financed from internal operations.

The repeatable unit is critical to scaling up. It's not enough to get your distribution channel to produce revenue; you must understand why it is working well so you can replicate it.

Incidentally, one of the reasons many fast-growing food companies can't sustain growth is because they don't really know, analytically, what they're doing right.

You need to understand your sales and marketing process at a numerical level, the way someone running a massive cookie factory line knows precisely how each segment of the line is performing at any second of any day.

Distribution Problem #2:

Your Distribution Channel's "Repeatable Unit" Shows Only Modest Performance

So, what happens if you're in a situation where the performance of your "repeatable unit" is mediocre? Your sales routes costs $120,000 but only produces $300,000. This is enough to put a little dent in your overhead but is not really a major contributor to your gross revenue. Or your recent consumer trade campaign shows that it costs you $1.00 to get a shopper to purchase your product, but you make only $1.20. It's a tiny profit hardly worth attempting to replicate on a wider scale.

Repeatedly, I share with food entrepreneurs in situations like these, you're better off not trying to replicate or scale up your distribution. In this case, your focus needs to be on two specific areas: troubleshooting your sales and marketing process and increasing your revenues per customer. I put the brakes on expanding distribution in hopes the increased revenue will fix the lack of massive profits. It's not a scale problem!

If your sales and marketing process is not performing well, you have to continually adjust it until you can get the numbers up to a level that's worth replicating. Here's how to do it.

Break down your sales and marketing process into specific steps: Measure the performance of each step, systematically A/B test each step of the sales and marketing process and look for the alternative that generates more sales.

I'll provide some examples in a second, but first, let me define an A/B test. In an A/B test, you alternate between two versions of a particular step in your sales and marketing process (e.g., package claims and branding content, promotions, direct mail pieces, demo scripts, taglines, online and social media messaging, etc.) and carefully track which one worked better.

This, frankly, is how 80% of all sales and marketing should be done. It should involve a systematic, analytical approach to continuously improving the results from your in-house distribution channel. Perry Marshall in his book 80/20 Rule in Business brilliantly maps out this process of testing and narrowing down to your best success. Let me share several examples for you to consider in your own business.

For one client in California, I reviewed their product portfolio and pricing structure. Once I completed the analytics it appeared we had a significant opportunity to introduce products and packages to consumers far beyond the sub-$10 price point. We introduced an $89 version and it began selling in days. We are now testing even higher priced products in the 3 and 4 figure price points with higher values for the shopper.

My client in Virginia also tested higher price points for her direct-to-consumer website and successfully transitioned her entire business from $40 retail product to $150 product and we are now looking at a $200+ and a custom $1,000 version of the $40 product. It all begins with testing. It's not just pricing but everything associated with the process of sales and marketing must be reviewed and tested.

This sounds like a pain to do, and it is, but it systematically and continuously increases revenues. The math is compelling, as evidenced in the following example.

The A/B Split-Testing Math:

How a 3% Weekly Improvement Generates 150% Annual Revenue Growth

One of the keys to creating and sustaining a Food Money Machine is to look for high return on investment opportunities in your business. These are opportunities that require only modest effort but increase revenues at a level substantially more than the effort required. Or, phrased differently, the key to Food Money Machine growth is to look for the "little hinges that swing big doors." A/B testing is, without question, one of the highest-leveraging revenue growth opportunities you have in your business. The math is exceptionally compelling.

Here's an example: Let's say you run a test every week in either a marketing campaign, product, or in your sales process. On average, you find one version outperforms another version by an average of only 3%. As far as A/B testing goes, this is a tiny level of improvement. It's common to get 15 to 20% improvement per attempt, particularly early on in the process.

You repeat the process of taking a new action or changing an element in your efforts again next week, and again the week after and so on for each week of the year. You will find some good improvements and other weeks there will be no improvement. If you stay with the process, you will generate a return over each week with your sales and marketing process. If you keep at it for 52 weeks or 104 weeks, you'll see a tremendous overall impact of 150% increase in sales for the year or two – with almost no additional costs in your marketing, it actually should cost less.

Not just marketing, but you can find areas throughout your business to leverage, exploit, test, and improve that when compounded with these small changes in sales and marketing will have massive impact on your business success. The areas I like to investigate include marketing, strategy, capital, business model, relationships, distribution channels, products, procedures, and even ideology of the team.

It's almost unimaginable the amount of exponential growth that can be found when seeking minor adjustments in multiple areas for success. If you can pick up a 5% improvement each week, you'll double revenues every four months. If you can get only a 1% improvement each week at the end of a year it will be a 50% increase in revenue. Details matter and we are not seeking home runs, but instead disciplined approaches to seeking daily wins throughout the months and years.

At this point, you can double your sales force or double your marketing effort every 12 months on a completely self-financed basis. By combining a 150% increase in revenues for each "repeatable unit" with a 100% increase in the number of "repeatable units," you're posting a 250% annual growth, year after year. So, if you can hit $1 million this year your run rate next year is $3.5 million with system improvements and duplication.

Having gone through these efforts repeatedly in my over two-decades consulting career, I know from experience the easy 10% to 30% growth hits can come easier in the early part of the process. As time progresses and testing continues, it gets harder and more difficult to find even a 5% improvement.

The point of these tests and my review is to illustrate that the key to improving the revenue productivity of the "repeatable unit" in your distribution channel is to continuously rack up a series of tiny wins. You do this by employing disciplined testing as part of every operation in your Food Money Machine.

Distribution Problem #3:

How to Expand Third-Party Distribution Partners

Show them the money! That's the most important thing to keep in mind when trying to scale up distribution through partners. Partners want to increase their revenues in a way that's consistent with their values and quality standards. The more you can match that, the more successful you'll be with partners.

In general, there are two ways you can show them more money. First, they can profit by reselling your products (or by you paying them a fee or commission). Second, you can show your partner how every time a customer buys one of your company's food products they automatically want to buy more of the partner's product or service.

In food categories, it's a relatively simple exercise to show retail, foodservice, leisure segment operators how they can benefit from adding food and your product to their category mix. In Chapter 7, we share an exception template and process on sharing your value equation with partners.

The classic example of selling desserts, you demonstrate to the restaurateur how valuable selling desserts to guests will be on his bottom-line. If only 10% of guests will add a dessert to the check it will have a massive impact on profits and guest satisfaction. So, either way, it's important you show partners a path to more money. Spell it out for them.

When a retailer or operator partner makes significantly more money partnering with you versus a competitor it becomes much easier to get more of them. Not only can you afford to invest more in partner acquisition, but you will also find that a higher percentage of prospective partners become actual partners. This, of course, accelerates your Food Money Maker and increases revenues from additional channels, which, in turn, provides you with even more resources to attract more partners. The process steadily cycles upward.

Distribution Problem #4:

How to Increase Revenues from the Distribution You Already Have

The key to maximizing revenues and profits from an existing distribution channel is straightforward: Sell them more stuff. Sell them more of your food products and sell them more of other people's stuff either in your brand or the supplier's brand.

Your effective margins on sales to existing customers will always be substantially higher than sales to new customers. So, selling more to existing customers drives top-line sales and improves bottom-line profit margins, all at the same time.

This seems like such a mundane way to increase food revenues. There's no magic bullet, no super-sexy partnership deal, no whiz-bang marketing campaign—just sell more to your existing customers.

In my advisory work with food clients, I routinely focus on this technique to generate an immediate surge in my client's food revenues. For smaller food clients with flat sales, I've repeatedly doubled revenues within the first year. It often is a very simple process. Let me share with you one example how I did this for Dyson Limited, a United Kingdom technology and vacuum company.

When approached by Dyson's business development specialist, I was intrigued with the idea of helping their division focused on restaurants to achieve massive growth and found it. In the first year, the division achieved an 83% growth from a very simple process.

Initially, I requested that Dyson all invoices for the prior 30 days. After review and much to my surprise the larger orders came from healthcare and the top client in the restaurant division was a hospital! I immediately built a database of all hospitals and healthcare facilities and emailed it to the group. The list generated massive growth and success in existing accounts already a part of distribution but lacked focus.

Here is another example that maximizes sales revenue from existing accounts – displays.

There is likely no better opportunity for Food Money Machines than building and deploying branded displays of your products into your customer and distribution channel segments. The display becomes a defector retailer within the retailer.

I've seen displays generate anywhere from 200% to 1,000% increase in sales volume and you do not have to deploy them into food stores. In many instances they work even better in locations that are not accustomed to merchandising your food product category.

One of my former employees went on to work for Mrs. Fields Cookies and we were discussing his best-selling locations for his cookie brand. Surprisingly, he shared that Best Buy was his brands #1 selling location nationwide. There were no other cookies in the set and employees along with shoppers would purchase his cookie at a higher sales rate per location than any convenience or supermarket in the country

So, here's the key rule to remember: When you have an established distribution channel and customer base, bring them more value, and use them often!

Key Ideas:

Distribution is one of the most trivialized, under-valued and under-utilized methods for Food Money Machine growth.

Until you have access to a prospective market and consumers, nothing else matters.

To dominate new customer acquisition in your market, lead your industry in revenues per customer. The company that makes the most per customer is the company that can afford to invest the most to secure their markets and get into new ones.

Whenever we expand distribution, focus on getting your distribution to work on a small scale (i.e., "constrain to scale"), document what you did right, and then add new markets with expectations and a clear business case for customers serving your avatar consumer markets.

It's not enough to grow fast, everyone thinks the solution is to expand distribution and add new channels quickly; you need to grow fast in a way that the model can be duplicated and multiplied. That's the difference between growth and sustained growth. You don't fix revenue and profit problems with scale. Food Money

Machine growth comes from disciplined focus on using test markets and test cases to generate tiny incremental improvements across many areas weekly, monthly, and quarterly that add up to significant growth over time.

To dominate retail and market distribution, provide partners with a well-honed sales message, valuable innovation for consumer markets, and drive traffic produced through A/B split testing, premium priced products, and a higher payout percentage—all of which puts more money into the distribution and retailer partner's pocket.

Know that at the end of the day, you are responsible for driving sales success with consumers in your partner markets.

CASE STUDY

CLUB STORE CHAMPION

Tim's innovative channel vision and alignment methods helped clients to introduce new products and brands to Costco and the club store channel. As a result, 22 new companies with no prior experience or sales in the club store channel experienced success through Tim's connections and direction. Tim's clients sold more than $60 million into club stores.

CHAPTER 5:

Food Money Machine Product

Food Money Maker Issues: The Food Product

The Food Money Maker is the foundation of all growth. A Food Money Maker is a specific market opportunity combined with your company's approach to capturing it.

A Food Money Maker Consists of Five Key Ingredients:

- A target consumer that recognizes she or he has a problem or need.

- A promise that your company makes to prospective shopper.

- A distribution channel for reaching and transacting business with the target shopper.

- A product that fulfills the promises made to the consumer.

- A sustainable competitive advantage.

In this chapter, I'm going to focus on potential issues surrounding the food product you are planning to manufacture. Creating Food Money Maker growth requires your company to produce food products that your customers love and that are easy to sell through your designated distribution channels.

If you noticed, this attribute is #4 on the list and of far less importance to creating your Food Money Maker than the other more relevant and important points to your shopper. It's all about consumer needs as compared to your recipe formulation and product development. It's about delivering on your promise.

Consumers love products that fix a problem or provide for some need. The key is creating products that fulfill the promises made to the shopper to generate the sale. In other words, your product needs to actually solve the problem you promised your shoppers you would solve. The first stage of developing a successful food product is generating ideas and brainstorming on problems you can solve for consumers. When framed in this manner the creation and development of a food product is much more involved than preparing a unusual dish, product, or sauce for friends and family or utilizing a new technological food ingredient.

Sounds simple—and you'd think it is—but it's shocking how often food products do an incomplete job of solving customers' problems. I've seen countless food products introduced and fail to gather market traction since they never actually solved a consumer's problem. The product was all about a great tasting and incredible formulation or some new ingredient and the artistry in the product itself.

Luck and outright copycat products are more common than you might ever imagine in the food business. It is not the path to Food Money Maker success and continued growth over time. Your business will require repeatable ongoing processes.

To assist with the product creation process, here are my top questions to ask as you progress on your food product development:

1. Does your product answer an unmet need?

2. How will you creatively brand your offer for this unmet need?

3. Which channel will consumers want to purchase this item?

4. Are your consumers searching for a solution or will you create impulse purchases?

5. How will you develop consumer awareness and connections?

6. How does your product perform against others in the current likely category?

After you've generated ideas, you will need to cull and prioritize the various problems you hope to promise a solution with your product. It will also be appropriate to begin considering how many people your solution will appeal to in the market. The goal is to avoid too small a market while finding a niche that will not lose money once you commercialize the product.

Your outline of markets and consumer problems will provide guidance to feasibility studies and the economics of each product. There are other general areas that you will review at this stage: production and technology concerns, any pertinent state and federal laws, and the financial plans and objectives.

In addition to asking questions, you should spend time auditing various retail locations along with researching online what is occurring in your specific category.

This article is not about how to build a product management and development organization—I'll have to save that for another time. It is, however, an article that describes the "big picture" principles that are absolutely essential for getting food product development and introductions "right."

Tim's Law of Food Product Development:

"Don't Create a Food Product unless it solves a Problem."

Here's a simple story that illustrates my point on product development: Keurig and the K-cup pods have found tremendous success and growth since their introduction over 20 years ago with their coffee products.

Their product development folks got busy and thought it would be great to develop a similar product for the cold carbonated beverages too. With Keurigs pedigree, it's easy to assume success with this winning opportunity.

Product development and consumer needs do not begin with engineering or even pre-built models. It's about solving problems for the market consumer and supplying an answer to their needs.

Keurig Kold cost $370 for a big clunky counter unit. The Coca-Cola modules cost $4.99 for a 4-pack that made 8 ounce glasses of Coke and the unit required constant running for hours before it was useable. It made loud humming noises while a 2 liter bottle of Coke retails for about $2 and off-brands sell for $1 per 2 liter bottle. What problem did the unit solve for consumers? It's an obvious failure when reviewed through the lens of consumer need that the product offers no solution but not so obvious when viewed as a technological advance and equivalent to the wildly successful coffee market.

Before building a food product, begin with the problem you are going to solve and how you are going to make life better for consumers that believe your promise and purchase your product. This start is the most productive and functional method to build terrific new food products for markets. The way we do this is beginning with our target consumer and their problems that we intend to promise a solution.

There is a lesson here. It's not about the new technology, culinary excellence, or product development know-how; it's about solving a consumer's problem. And you can't do that unless you and your team fully understand the problem in great detail and show empathy for their situation and consumers result.

The Food Product Development Process:

Simple Acid Tests:

How to Tell if Your Product Development Team Is Doing It Right

Here are some simple acid tests to determine if your product development team is doing things right.

Ask your development team these questions: What's the first and last name of an actual person who typifies the target consumer or prospective customers we're trying to satisfy with our new food product?(Hint: The wrong answer is no answer.)How many "team hours" do you estimate will be required for this product development? How many hours have we spent with actual consumers and prospective shoppers making sure we understand the problems we're trying to solve with our latest food product? Are we comfortable with this ratio?

On this last point, you'd be shocked at some of the ratios I've seen in food companies. It is not uncommon to find zero hours interacting with real bonifide consumers and customers to actually understand their problems and how a food company might address and add value to their lives.

Product Development Tips

If all you do is follow "Tim's Rule of Food Product Development— Build Products that Solve Consumer Problems," your company will have better product development processes than 90% of other food companies.

Every incremental hour, day, and week spent to really under-stand the consumer and the consumer's problems is exceptionally worthwhile. A keen understanding of consumers and their problems will enable you to focus your product development resources on solving the problems that matter most. This leads to greater shopper satisfaction, market success, and better sales results.

The following are other common product development problems and how to fix them.

Product Development Tip #1:

Features Should Be Aligned with Food Money Machine growth.

Product development's role is not to produce added features; it's to enable Food Money Machine growth in a way that happens to involve building features specific to a consumer promise and channel need.

It is better to deliver all of the requirements for one channel opportunity than to fulfill half of the requirements for two channels. While both approaches use the same research and development resources, the first approach has a higher revenue growth impact.

For each food product launch, start by prioritizing the distribution channels (not the features). The number one priority revenue growth channel should be complete before we begin building products for the number two priority growth channel.

By shifting the focus from product development to prioritizing revenue growth channels first, you'll find that food product development is much more aligned with driving revenue growth

Product Development Tip #2:

Do the research. Is the product already on the market?

You would be surprised how many people approach me each year with a product or what they considered an innovative food concept and it's already on the market. Worse, the product has been introduced to the market and it failed.

Visit tradeshows, seek out specialty stores, visit super-markets and other food retailers, visit online food retailers, and investigate with store audits and Google searches. It's important you understand the category and any success or lack of success in your category for a similar product.

If you find the food product is already on the market or has experienced a failed launch, the information is valuable. You can seek out data for how you might change or manage the food product introduction process for your product. It may reflect a new sensitivity to pricing and business models. It also might suggest your product is innovative with a potential loyal consumer following but the market is too small and you will lose money trying to introduce your product.

How to Tell if Your Product Development Team Is Doing It Right

In my food consulting career, I've been involved in literally 100's of new product developments, launches, test markets, and line enhancements. I've also had the enormous advantage of working with the largest food brands in the world and help launch multiple zero revenue food concepts to million dollar winners – so, I've seen an incredible volume of food product launches and the resulting impact.

This has allowed me to see how a simple decision in food product development ripples through the to the sales and marketing organization and, ultimately, to the channel and consumer.

In addition, my diverse experience gives me the ability to listen and research for what I consider the key points in product development that make for a successful Food Money Machine.

As an example: within the first seven minutes of speaking with a food entrepreneur I can often figure out if his product and company will have what is necessary to achieve massive food success. At that point, it's a natural feeling that I can interpret based on the questions and answers in our discussion. I can do this because good and bad food development processes are readily apparent in discussion and in the product itself.

Usually, my first question is "How did you arrive at creating this food product?" I also like to ask food entrepreneurs "How did you get into the food business?"

Then by listening, looking at any product information, and the company's website I'll gain additional information or support of my observations. Just by looking at the label and visiting their sites you can tell an awful lot about a food product organization's collective beliefs, habits, and processes or lack thereof.

A customer-oriented food team will create a product package that's intuitive to the end user's needs. They often come to me with small individual market success stories, consumer interviews and descriptions of how the product serves a need for consumers in a channel.

In contrast, a research and development oriented product development organization will design the food product in the exact opposite way. The underlying food product will be created first, often by a research chef, and a brand or label will be slapped on as an afterthought.

Closing Thoughts

Use these food product development Chapter lines and you will create food products that are easier to sell and that your consumers will really love. Don't forget that all of these tips stem from my golden rule of product development: "Don't Build a Food Product unless it solves a Problem."

Key Ideas:

Tim's Rule of Food Product Development: You Can't Build a Product to Solve a Problem You Don't Understand Test the effectiveness of your product development team by asking to see a list of the consumers they spoke to before they came up with the current product design. It's better to complete 100% of the features needed to get one channel to take off than to complete 50% of the features for two channels. The promise IS the product and should be designed before the food product is crafted.

CASE STUDY

FOOD NETWORK PROMISE

Tim created a massive growth engine for Fondarific with no change to the product recipe formula. The only change was to the name and promise made to a new distribution channel of consumers. Tim authored the trade campaign, set pricing strategy, developed a national plan, tradeshow program and introduced Fondarific to the Food Network. The result was moving from the clients backyard shed to a new production facility with 30 employees, millions in revenue and an SBA Small Business of the Year Award!

CHAPTER 6:

Food Money Machine - Competitive Advantage

The Food Money Maker is the foundation of all growth. A Food Money Maker is a specific market opportunity combined with your company's approach to capturing it.

A Food Money Maker Consists of Five Key Ingredients:

1. A target consumer who's aware of his or her problem.
2. A promise that your company makes to prospective consumer.
3. A distribution channel for reaching and transacting with the target shopper.
4. A product or service that fulfills the promise made to the customer.
5. A sustainable competitive advantage.

In this article, I'm going to discuss issues with the fifth, and final, component of a Food Money Maker: the sustainable competitive advantage. A sustainable competitive advantage is a "soft" or "hard" asset that's difficult for a competitor to duplicate. This enables you to extend the lifespan of your Food Money Maker.

A soft asset might be a product development process capable of producing new food product revisions in only four months, while the rest of the industry takes seven months. Another soft asset might be a method of recruiting and interviewing that consistently attracts exceptionally gifted employees.

A hard asset could be a patent on a unique product design, a manufacturing facility, or a refrigerated warehouse.

Here's an example of why creating a sustainable competitive advantage, while growing revenues, is so important:

Sustainable Competitive Advantages Enable Sustained Revenue Growth

We discussed briefly direct to store delivery and this has been a source of sustainable competitive advantage for one leading snack food and potato chip company in the United States.

Frito-Lay has built up an efficient dsd delivery system that can reach the smallest of retail outlets and channels. It uses small step-van trucks that take small order to small outlets like gas stations, convenience stores and drug stores. It has built an efficient delivery system of depots and routes that allows it to do this economically.

This direct approach and visiting the locations provides Frito with enormous advantage compared to other snack food companies with what goes on the shelf, how much shelf space they end up with in-store and the amount of special displays and secondary marketing opportunities they receive with retail stores.

The company is very focused on their distribution system and you will not see beverages or heavy products or larger bulky consumer products on their trucks that slow down their delivery efficiency.

The result has been a competitive advantage against other snack food companies and offers them a much higher unit sales rate at very attractive margins. It's important to note that many of their products are me-too and not unique.

Frito-Lays distribution system is one of their competitive advantages.

Leverage a Competitive Advantage or Create One

There are two types of Food Money Makers; small ones and big ones. A small Food Money Maker might be a particular one-time-only promotion to your existing customers. It's a growth engine with a limited lifespan but one that's acknowledged and accepted. These "low hanging fruit" opportunities can boost a company's revenues with unusually low risk. However, the lifespan of these opportunities is often measured in weeks or months.

The second type of Food Money Maker is the big ones—cracking open new markets, going after a new customer segment, or solving a new class of problems for your existing customer base. The investment of time, money, and resources in the pursuit of these opportunities ranges from "significant" on the low end to "bet the company" on the high end.

For these types of Food Money Maker opportunities, the role of the competitive advantage is important to consider. Each major growth engine should either take advantage of an existing competitive advantage or create one as a byproduct.

The reason for this is that the sustainability of your revenue growth engine is directly tied to your competitive advantages. If your pursuit of a revenue growth engine doesn't involve using or creating a competitive advantage, competitors can duplicate your efforts easily. This shortens the lifespan of the opportunity and makes it nearly impossible to sustain extreme revenue growth.

In contrast, when you leverage an existing competitive advantage as part of your growth engine it makes it difficult for a competitor to copy you. We are seeing this in category after category in the food sector.

One of the most dismaying trends of all for large, mega-brand food companies is that scale is losing its value. Small   brands are able to compete effectively by outsourcing manufacturing and other business functions while developing supplier relationships with big chains that sell to a large part of the ACV market. In fact, many retail supermarket chains are actively pursuing relationships with smaller brands to appeal to changing consumer preferences.

This is the key for creating extreme revenue growth that's sustainable over the long haul. You must either link revenue growth engines to exploit your existing competitive advantages or incorporate the creation of competitive advantages into your revenue growth plans. Either way, the sustainable competitive advantage is the key for long-term growth.

Purchase and Invest for Competitive Advantage

Competitive advantage is also important to company valuation and the future life of your food business. In recent years I've seen as many as 400 mergers and acquisitions in the food business. It's fascinating and interesting to see the reasoning and models these food companies are using to justify these expansions and sell-offs. We all are aware of consolidation but with the challenges from upstart brands, there is more effort placed into production and product capabilities.

- Common Corporate Purchase Strategies in the Food Industry

- Product or Category Relatedness

- Geographic Expansion

- Consolidation

- Innovation Acquisition

- Company

- Capability

Ultimately, Food Money Makers achieve market share and sustain competitive advantage making them ripe targets for purchase by capability-building suitors or those searching for valuable and special food businesses to operate.

Key Ideas:

How long you can sustain revenue growth is directly tied to your competitive advantages and how difficult it is for a competitor to copy them. (The Frito-Lay stepvan success) Every Food Money Maker opportunity should: exploit a pre-existing competitive advantage, create a new competitive advantage or enhance a pre-existing advantage, or both. This is the only sure way to sustain growth over the long term.

CASE STUDY

$16 MILLION INVESTMENT

Zaycon Fresh enlisted Tim to help with preparation of this privately-owned company's valuation. Tim assessed the firm's value based on the foundational five ingredients, demonstrated future value, and advised on efforts to raise financing for the company's food business. The end result was success on Wall Street and $16 million dollars in new capital.

CHAPTER 7:

Communicating Extreme Value

Food is likely the most competitive business niche in all of industry. There are massive limits on the use of intellectual property and the hoped for gains in a competitive advantage seem to more quickly vanish than in most other business segments due to the size and nature of competition in food.

This formidable field has developed practices and processes over the past 100 years to quickly build extreme food growth and discontinue item after item each year. The largest and biggest brands understand this need for information and context when sharing value with high growth partners.

In this quick recap, I'll share the plug-and-play formulas used by the best food brands to reach their goals in the food business. You might think it's simply a larger budget but it's actually nothing more than providing value, information, and context. The biggest established food corporations gain authorization after authorization growing their business with a proven method of sharing product value.

Innovative brands with a desire for extreme food revenue growth can follow suit. How do I know? I've competed with and beaten the largest brands in the world with their own playbook.

For example...

My startup client, Georgia Olive Farms was inspired while in Italy to develop an East coast olive oil and introduce it to the US market. They entered the market by adjusting to authenticity, disrupted the market by initially focusing on chefs, and became recognized as one of the best in America by the writers at the Wall Street Journal. Today, Georgia Olive Farms has over 100,000 olive trees and they are growing significant consumer sales revenue.

Nadine had a recipe and we met at her kitchen table to discuss plans. She quickly developed her chicken salad into a multi-million dollar business by using systems and strategies of the most successful food brands.

These entrepreneurial startup brands utilized the action steps the largest global food companies use to communicate with buyers in markets. The systems and process of communicating value are what helped them achieve their massive success.

The steps are repeatable and scalable formulas and processes. If you don't know them, you likely will not figure it out without much experience and many seasons of trial and error. I've identified them as the 9 Pillars of Big Food Brand Success.

The following lists the 9 Pillars and a brief discussion of their practice. Your brand will benefit from organizing and sharing value around these 9 areas of action. 9 Pillars of Communication for Extreme Food Revenue Growth

Product Innovation:

First and foremost, your food product will find extreme revenue growth when it connects with an unmet and recognized consumer need. Innovation is defined by a purchasing market and food makers ignore this fact!

Creative Execution:

Demonstrate an understanding of your consumer markets with packaging creative, programs, promotions, and online. You should offer insight into your market with Moms, Dads, Kids, or other groups of people in the most likely consumer demographic and psychographic markets for your product brand.

Customer Centric:

How does your company and product resonate with ideal consumers? Demonstrate how your product resonates in the life of your avatar consumer.

Consumer Insights:

Provide your partners with Consumer Characteristics and Use of Products. These communications might include Third party Research, Surveys, Demos, Emails, and Ask Customers surveys.

Retail Insights:

Give Direction to Retailer on your food product — Best Methods from other Retailer Success, Seasonality, Great Promo Ideas, Any Prior Experiences, Trials, Marketing Best Practices.

Consumer Connected:

Show buyer your current Consumer Connections with Testimony, Email, Sales, social media success stories.

Strong Brand:

Demonstrate the Power of your Brand and Performance with Customer success stories, Retailers, Dollars, Share, Success in Market, and Competitive Retailers.

Traffic Builder:

How will you drive business to the store and into the department for your product? There are cost-effective and local methods for this that include coupons, advertisements, social media, emails, and customer engagement.

Business Case:

Surprisingly, I rarely have a client that has ever presented a business case to a significant retailer before working together. They don't understand that this is seen as missing from their presentation by buyers. You have to demonstrate and provide an explanation of your products financial impact to the category. Guess what? If you don't do this, your largest competitors will have loads of data to share about your lack of success and low numbers with your retail partner.

Present your case for why you should be authorized, demonstrate with credibility your financial impact on category revenue, sales and profits. Discuss share, unit movement and expected results.

Extreme fast growing and largest food brands utilize these effective strategies year after year to achieve continued success. They leverage their current position and markets for growth. It's not just budget but process that garners the results for these food businesses. Regardless of size or spend, you can achieve extreme food growth utilizing these nine practices.

Extreme food revenue growth requires you to apply the 9 Pillars in your presentations, market efforts, and programs for retailers, distributors, partners, and customers.

Key Ideas:

The world's leading food brands and consumer product goods makers communicate with buyers utilizing a system to communicate value. The points that leading brands communicate with retail and foodservice partners can be utilized by smaller entrepreneurial brands for growth and success. The 9 areas of partner value include innovative products, creative execution, consumer concentric, consumer insights, retailer insights, consumer connections, brand strength, traffic builder, and business case.

CASE STUDY

BELL RINGING SUCCESS!

Blue Bell Creameries broke all sales records through a successful sales team event, after utilizing Tim's insights and strategies. The resulting sales numbers were the largest in the company history. In the 30-day period, more than 2 million consumers participated in this special promotion.

CHAPTER 8:

The 10 Times Systems Test

The first challenge every food entrepreneur faces is, "How do I get this food company to grow?" Once you solve this problem, the second challenge is, "Wow! How do we keep up with all this growth?" Sure, it's a great problem to have, but make no mistake about it—it really is a problem that needs to be solved.

Scalable Systems

The key for managing rapid food growth is to standardize your operations and design internal procedures that are scalable. Scalable operational procedures can handle significant increases in volume without re-design.

If you have a highly technical background, you'll recognize that these terms come from the technical side of the IT business. A scalable technology system is one that allows you to add many more users to your system without the system breaking under extreme usage.

A simple example would be your website and provider, such as Wordpress or Shopify. These platforms are fantastic systems designed for up to a specific amount of users and customers to shop on the page at any one time.

However, if you land on Shark Tank and 10,000 consumers attempt to check-out at the same time, it's going to break. The site is likely not designed to handle that heavy a load in the system. You might have a great looking and capable site, it's just not set-up to handle the 10,000 shoppers.

You will need to talk to your suppliers and internet provider on the capacity and ability of your site to take plenty of orders in such an event. Also, be sure to look for pieces of the process that might break with such a heavy load such as credit card processing, various systems, and plug-ins along with the amount of bandwidth your provider has allocated for your service.

Scalable "People" Systems

This concept of a "scalable system" can also be applied to the non-technical aspects of a food business. Every facet of your company - accounting, sales, marketing, customer service, consulting, product fulfillment, production, and technical support—is a system. I'm not talking about just the baking or tech systems used in these areas; I'm also talking about all the manual work that gets done.

For example, when you integrate a new employee into your company, you use a system. There are specific steps that need to be done—employee orientation, tax forms, employee benefit setup, e-mail address setup, provision of a desk, phone number assignment, and so on.

The key idea here is to recognize that literally everything in your business is, or should be, a system.

The "Bottleneck" Concept

An important concept to understand in dealing with systems is "the bottleneck." It's the part of the system that holds back every other part of the system. Executives who manage factories commonly use this term. When a portion of a manufacturing line is broken, it creates a bottleneck that constrains the output of the entire factory.

For example, let's say you were running an ice cream manu-facturing facility capable of producing 1,000 cartons of ice cream a day. One day, the carton sealer on the production line has a problem—one of the two primary sealing tools has failed, and only 500 cartons can be sealed a day, instead of 1,000.

This is the bottleneck.

Bottlenecks can cripple any system. In our example, ice cream production drops from 1,000 cartons per day to 500 cartons per day because of a single failure in the line.

It does not matter if the factory employs thousands of workers and every other part of the line is running at full capacity; the entire output of the facility is constrained by this single bottleneck.

Another way to characterize the bottleneck is: A system can only produce at the capacity of its weakest link.

The "Bottleneck" Is Enemy Number One

The Bottleneck effect has important implications when it comes to creating and sustaining extreme food revenue growth. It's impossible to sustain extreme revenue growth if you're not actively anticipating, looking for, and removing, the key bottlenecks in your company.

Let me give you some examples that illustrate this idea: Let's say your company has grown quite dramatically from $35 million in sales one year to $100 million the next. Clearly, your sales force was able to produce $100 million in sales. But, can your production and retailer order support departments handle $100 million in sales? If not, your customers will be disappointed in the experience. If the problem is severe enough, they will stop buying and your sales will automatically drop to a level your plant and retailer order support staff can handle. The market has a tendency to automatically correct itself whenever you have a bottleneck in your customer-interaction systems.

Obviously, you don't want the market demand to be reduced to meet your company's ability to supply. You'd much rather increase your company's ability to supply to meet the hot market demand. Now, in a modestly growing company (say 15% per year), this is much less of an issue. It's much easier for modestly growing businesses to improve their systems and capacity incrementally. The challenge in a company with extreme food revenue growth is the need for greater capacity —yesterday.

The Key to Scalable Systems: Remove the Bottleneck

The key to creating scalable operations is to continually look for, and anticipate, bottlenecks in your business operations, and to continually remove bottlenecks through process re-design, automation, or outsourcing. It's an on-going battle that you must deal with for as long as you intend to grow. In other words, you're always going to be dealing with this issue.

Remember, any time a system has a bottleneck it constrains the overall output of the system. So, if your capacity to recruit new employees is lower than your ability to generate revenues, you're going to hit a brick wall at some point. If your website can handle 10 million users a day, but your bandwidth agreements and data storage systems only allow 1 million users a day, when user number 1,000,001 visits the site there are going to be problems.

Here's the peculiar thing about bottlenecks: They're often hidden and difficult to detect. It's also common for underlying bottlenecks to be far removed from their more visible consequences. For example, if you had a slowdown in sales, would it ever occur to you that the reason is due to the lack of customer service reps for your club store channel? So, what are you supposed to do? Go answer phones for the reps yourself? Of course not.

Here's an easier approach. Train your team and all your employees to be on the lookout for future bottlenecks and eliminate them before they can constrain growth. You will have to remind your team to do this constantly. It takes a little more effort up front to create a process, procedure, or system that scales well, but it makes such a big difference in the end.

The 10 Times Test

A simple way to get your entire team thinking about and removing future bottlenecks is to ask them a simple question: "If our business grew 10 times overnight, would you be able to handle it?"

Ask your head of Customer Service: "If our new customer volume increased by tenfold, tomorrow morning at 9 a.m., would your department be able to handle it?

Ask your appointment desk, dock, and warehouse: "If the number of trailers needing full pallets increased 10 times, could you handle the number of loads?"

Your VP of Sales should be thinking: "If the number of retailer category reviews and promotional interest increased tenfold by 9:00 tomorrow morning, could my team follow up with all of them?"

Don't be surprised if the first time you ask these questions you get a "You're crazy" look. In spite of the look, it is the right question to ask. In fact, from a "managing growth" perspective, it is THE question to ask.

Here's why: It gets your team thinking about all the ripple effect issues that 10 times growth would cause.

We'll take a simple example: If your customer service department had to handle a 10 times growth in new customers each month, could they do it? If not, why? Let's look at the potential issues: We don't have enough customer service agents—we'd need at least 6 more. Of course, we'd need 6 new computers. But, wait. Can we get

6 computers overnight? Even if we got them, can our IT service set up 6 computers overnight? We need desks. Of course, people need desks...and chairs! We don't have the office space to house 6 new customer service agents. Could we build out space in the warehouse? Is that an option? Trailer in the lot? What's the lead time required for getting more office space? It has to be 90 to 180 days to get good terms. Wait. Do we have anyone focused on our real estate needs? This seems like a nightmare. Should we outsource our customer service to a third party or public warehouse that already manages 150 times more volume than we do? Or, should we set up an "overflow" agreement with a third-party co-packer that automatically kicks in during our busy periods? But, is customer service something we need to control directly, or is it a non-core activity? Would these customer service requests come in by e-mail or edi? Will our edi supplier handle the new order volume and accounts?—If by email, can our team handle the email requests? Oh yeah, if the requests came in by rep, our rep case-tracking system would fail, too—we'd need to upgrade to the deluxe version of that system. Ugh, how would we train these new agents? Right now, we

use a "buddy system" that pairs up a new agent with a veteran agent for a month or two. We can't have new agents training new agents, and we can't have each veteran agent mentor 2 new agents simultaneously. Should we move to a training course format? Would a self-directed eLearning training process scale better? Can we make screen capture videos to automatically train customer service? How would we manage all these employees? We'd need a new layer of management, for sure. How would we staff it? What would be the ratio of "team leader" to customer service agent?

I always measure how good a question is by how many other questions it inspires. By this measure, the "10 Times Test" is a really good question.

So, ask yourself: "Could my company handle 10 times growth overnight?"

Almost every time I've asked this question I've gotten a frown in response. That's because virtually every leader I know realizes the answer to the question is "No."

Further, the question itself shines a bright light on all the potential bottlenecks.

It forces you to answer the questions about what parts of your business would "break" under a 10 times increase in business.

More importantly, you want your entire team thinking about what could be done today (with little to no incremental cost) that would make it easier to handle such growth.

The key to managing, and ultimately sustaining, extreme food revenue growth is to anticipate future revenue growth bottlenecks and eliminate them before they actually constrain revenue growth.

Key Ideas:

A system that is scalable is one that can handle enormous surges in volume or usage without falling apart. This term applies to people-powered systems as well as technology systems. The key to getting a system scalable is to remove bottlenecks that slow down the performance of a system. Revenue generation is a system too—a system that is also constrained by bottlenecks. Your entire company should be focused on anticipating, finding, and eliminating bottlenecks that constrain revenue growth. The 10 Times Test: If your food revenues increased by 10 times overnight, would your company be able to handle it or would your systems "break"?

CASE STUDY

Rite Aid had a problem. Tim showed Rite-Aid Drugs how to keep the same promise and product offering for consumers during the merger of KB Drugs with RITE-AID.

RITE-AID had purchased KB Drugs, a regional chain with 200 locations in six Southern states. At the time, KB produced a regional-favorite line of ice creams, however the ice cream plant would not be part of the Rite Aid purchase. Tim's strategies helped Rite Aid avoid conflict and successfully consolidate the regional KB chain into the national Rite Aid organization. In this case, the promise and store brand remained unchanged in the new RITE-AID locations.

CHAPTER 9:

The Extreme Food Revenue Jump Start Session

All of the examples and scenarios in the Food Money Machine series of articles have come from my work and "Food Money Machine" sessions with clients. I've lived growing food enterprises for more than three decades.

If you are serious about your Food Company achieving or sustaining extreme revenue growth—growing your sales by 100% or more in the next twelve months—then I would encourage you to contact my office to be considered for a session.

I will work with you to identify and focus your attention on the two or three actions you can take to trigger extreme revenue growth in your food company over the next twelve months. The emphasis is not on creating a laundry list of things to do to grow your company. The focus is on finding the one, two or, at most, three most important, lowest cost, and easiest to implement actions you can take to drive dramatic increases in food revenues. Here's the idea behind these sessions:

In every food business, there is always an unpolished diamond with untapped market revenue potential. It's in virtually every business. Its untapped value is often overlooked or taken for granted by those who see it every single day.

As an outsider with fresh eyes, it takes me anywhere from twenty minutes to two hours to find these unpolished diamonds. During the rest of the time, I'll show you how I've helped others dig it up, polish it, and make more money from it. We will find new ways to add value to your food enterprise.

In other words, I find the most profitable opportunity inside your food company, and I show you how to extract your time, money, and people away from the

slower growth projects, shifting them to the highest growth opportunity within ninety days or less.

Of course, it is not possible for every food company to achieve extreme revenue growth. Because of this, I have a fairly rigorous screening process for selecting which clients I'll take on for an "Food Money Maker Jump Start" session. I do so because I want to be certain that my clients will get value from these sessions.

The promise of finding just one to three actions you can take to double your sales in twelve months is a big promise. I advise my clients to make as big and unique a promise as they possibly can while still being able to deliver. I practice what I preach and do the same with my advisory work.

However, the reality is there are certain types of clients and client situations where I know in advance, I will not be able to deliver on this promise. So, to protect my track record and reputation, I decline these requests for the benefit of everyone involved.

This also gives the clients I do accept the confidence that, despite the substantial fees involved with these sessions, they will get more than their money's worth.

To receive a free extreme food growth workbook and application for my "Food Money Maker Jump Start" session, visit my website or send an email:

www.timforrestmarkets.com

CASE STUDY

TIM CREATES A VOCATIONAL FOOD SCHOOL IN CALCUTTA, INDIA

Amlan Ganguly, Director of Prayasam, dreamed of a commercial catering company that the children in the slums of Calcutta, India could operate for experience and graduate to skilled positions in restaurants and hospitality including owning their own enterprise. In 2015, Tim in cooperation with Amlan and with the help of chefs and others built a vocational food school in Calcutta, India.

CHAPTER 10:

Resources for Outstanding Food Revenue Success

I hope you've found this book to be a useful resource and inspiration for propelling your food company's journey toward outstanding food revenue success.

It's important to keep in mind that extraordinary food revenue growth is not a one-time activity—it's an on-going process.

To ensure that you continually receive the most current and up-to-date tools, methodologies, and processes, I will be publishing free updates, bonus chapters, reports, audios, and videos related to these articles on my website.

Sign-up to download these free bonus items, and to be notified of future free updates, simply visit my website: **www.timforrest.com**

Closing Comments

It's been a pleasure discussing food success, a topic I'm passionate about. I wish you well in your extraordinary food revenue success adventures and encourage you to use the tools that you've discovered in this book.

I do have a favor to ask you. I would like to know what you thought of this book and would welcome any comments or suggestions you might have for me. It would be awesome if you send a quick note by emailing me at **www.timforrest.com.** I plan to use your feedback to improve and refine my plans for future books, articles, videos, and resources. I'm always looking to improve!

Finally, I want to wish you the best of luck in achieving extraordinary food revenue success in your company.

Tim Forrest
tim@timforrest.com

CASE STUDY

GEORGIA™
OLIVE
FARMS
LAKELAND, GEORGIA

Tim Forrest Leads First-Time Olive Growers To Nationally Recognized Olive Oil Brand in 18 Months. When the Shaw family decided to get into olive oil marketing in 2009, they had little experience in the consumer product business. They were successful and talented farmers with a dream of getting into the consumer product business, something that was completely new to them. They needed someone with all-round expertise in cpg, marketing, branding and distribution. Someone who has a great track record of delivering both the big perspective tasks (like channel selection, sales protocols, distribution) and the smaller building blocks (like labelling, UPC codes and FDA rules), and skillfully piecing them all together. They wanted to shorten the learning curve and avoid the big mistakes that new entrants can't afford to make.

The Shaws Get Their Task List Cut Out

"Biggest challenge was that we were starting from nothing", says Jason Shaw.

Olives had not been grown here in over 200 years. They had set their eyes on growing their domain beyond farming, and into building a successful consumer brand of olive oil.

With Tim's guidance, they identified their top goals:

1. Discover their core olive oil consumers.
2. Review and determine the key distribution channels for their market.
3. Create a differentiated product message
4. Create a brand design and package that demonstrates the superior Georgia Olive Farms olive oil for core consumers and selected channels.

"We had to prove ourselves to other growers", says Jason. "We had no experience in trying to market our own brand", says Shaw. He adds, "we were looking for someone who was willing to grow with us, and to offer ground-up type support." That's when they learned about Tim Forrest.

They did their research about Tim's work and learned about the results he had produced for some of the largest food brands in the world. The Shaws knew they had their man: "Tim had the knowledge level and all we had to do was listen to him and put the plans into action." He adds, "other consultants were just specific, but Tim could help with everything."

Tim Forrest Elevates Georgia Olive Oil With His Brand Paradigm and Focus on Distribution Channels.

The four partners started working under the guidance of Tim Forrest. They had frequent face-to-face meetings, and swiftly rolled out their plans. "[Tim] He could always be here if we needed him", says Jason. Tim set the best channel opportunities and distribution targets.

He dropped their focus and sales efforts with the super-market channel as well as tactics of building giant case displays in the larger national chains and regional grocery chains. He applied his experience and insight for Georgia Olive Farms by getting them up to speed while avoiding the many pitfalls of navigating in new areas. Jason says, "He [Tim] laid out a marketing plan that would work from the beginning."

There were many Italian olive oil brands in the market, and it was important not to get lost in the crowd. The packaging design also had to impart the distinction of a better product. Tim led the design effort and managed the creative agency. The market took to it and the brothers were happy about the creative outcome: local, bold, classy and at the same time international. Tim led the creation of a family of products, price points, and names that worked for their chosen distribution markets. Tim also tapped his network of business associates, many of whom became retail partners of the olive brand. Tim assisted obtaining favorable media exposure from Esquire Magazine, Food Channel, The Wall Street Journal, The Huffington Post, The Washington Post, Food Network, The Olive Oil Times, Garden and Gun Magazine. Jason says, "High-end chefs were educating consumers that led to more media exposure." Jason admits that they sold out of olive oil several times. "We are the only source for local olive oil on the entire east coast", he adds.

The Southern Revival Records show that in the 18th century, Spanish colonists on the coast of Georgia planted olive groves that persisted until sometime around the Civil War. Fast forward to 2009, when Georgia Olive Farms, a cooperative of growers from the southern part of the state began experimenting with different varieties. Their Arbequina, Arbesana and Koroneiki trees have since proven remarkably successful. The cooperative's Chef's Blend Extra Virgin Olive Oil is an excellent everyday oil with a mild, nutty flavor that works well for everything from sautéing vegetables to making hummus or drizzled on a wonderful salad.

Georgia Olive Farms, with Tim's help, achieved: - two successful olive oil products - Arbequina Extra Virgin Olive Oil and the Chef's Blend Extra Virgin Oil - brand acceptance by core market, resulting in significant cash flow in a market untainted by competition; - fast profitable growth without dealing with many of the issues and problems associated with going into the wrong channel; and strong public exposure.

Tim has decades of food marketing and distribution experience. He strategized, modified and simplified many processes. Georgia Olive Farms moved forward with speed while avoiding the pitfalls of navigating in new areas.

Talking about working with Tim, Jason says: "It gave you a peace of mind of having Tim to back me up. He stops what he's doing when you need him." Jason says, "we've already met our short-term goals, and now we are working on our long-term goals. Tim has been a key to our success. I hope to continue to keep working with Tim as long as we do this." Georgia Olive Farms, with Tim's guidance, completes our projects on time and on budget. When asked about recommending Tim Forrest, Jason Shaw was quick to say: "Oh heck ya, I've recommended."

ACKNOWLEDGEMENTS

I'm blessed, thankful and grateful for the consideration, leadership, love and acceptance shown by so many that made this book possible.

Family, mentors, friends, colleagues, advisors, and clients provided the necessary ingredients to capture and share these insights.

Traci, Sarah, Rhiannon, Hunter, John, Adam, Katen, Nathan, Todd Forrest, Lee and Gaye Forrest

I am grateful for the mentors and leaders that inspired and guided my efforts with their work: Blair Dunkley, Chris Frolic, Phil Symchych, David Ogilvie, Dan Weedin, Gary Furr, Dean Robinson and Suhani Vaidya.

This book could not exist without Steve Nelson and his Dad, my first food mentor - Lyle Nelson.

I extend my appreciation to Hazel Importante and Lynn McClurg for their massive impact and keeping so much in my work life on track.

Amlan Ganguly, Mugisha "The Lion," David Klein, Wally Amos, Justin Credible, Dee and Kenn Nilsen, Jo and her team, and Sharon Holmes.

Nunzio and Amanda Armanno, Bruce Bradford, Mike Irwin, Mike Keller, Chuck Lamkin, David Martin, Joe Melendez, Mike Myslinski, Pete Reed, Gary Roseman, Rick Wilshe and Randall Montalbano.

I owe special thanks to the clients and brands that demonstrated the impact and effectiveness of my ideas: Jason Shaw and team, Dan Oliver, Lauryn Chun, Tiffany Perkins, Jared Perkins, Plant Perks, Alex Hitz, Costco Wholesale and so many others including Adan and Yasmin Ventura, John Kalfayan, Pless and Elizabeth Jones, Dick Byne, Jeff Sheehan, Nadine Wardenga, Alex Hitz, The Food Network, and Walt Disney Company.

Lastly, I am grateful to food makers, food brands and strivers everywhere, who constantly search to deepen their knowledge, advance their markets, improve their companies, and make the world a healthier, tastier and more prosperous place for us all.

Author Contact Information

Website: **www.timforrest.com**

Newsletter: https://www.timforrest.com/contact-us/

Schedule a Meeting: www.timforrestmarkets.com

Email: tim@timforrest.com

EVERYONE'S Got a Recipe...5 Proven Ingredient to Scale Food Makers to Millions © 2023

Timothy Forrest

Printed in Great Britain
by Amazon

21396279R00079